Ultimate MOVIE SHOWSTOPPERS

MW00522945

Project Managers: Carol Cuellar and Donna Salzburg
Art Design: Ken Rehm
Text By: Fucini Productions, Inc.
Special thanks to David, Larry, Gail, Vincent, Mike, and Ken for their creative input

CONTENTS

Title	Movie	Page
All for Love	The Three Musketeers	16
American Pie	The Next Best Thing	9
Beautiful Stranger	Austin Powers: The Spy Who Shagged Me	22
Because You Loved Me	Up Close & Personal	29
Best Years of Our Lives	Shrek	34
Born to Be Wild	Easy Rider	41
Can't Fight the Moonlight	Coyote Ugly	44
A Certain Smile	A Certain Smile	49
Change the World	Phenomenon	62
Come What May	Moulin Rouge	52
Diamonds Are Forever	Diamonds Are Forever	59
Don't Say You Love Me	Pokémon—The First Movie	66
Endless Love	Endless Love	72
The Entertainer	The Sting	288
A Fool in Love	Meet the Parents	77
For the First Time	One Fine Day	82
For You I Will	Space Jam	88
Goldfinger	Goldfinger	93
The Greatest Love of All	The Greatest	96
The Green Mile (End Title)	The Green Mile	100
Have You Ever Really Loved a Woman?	Don Juan DeMarco	104
How Do I Live	Con Air	110
I Believe I Can Fly	Space Jam	114
I Can See Clearly Now	Cool Runnings	119
I Could Not Ask for More	Message in a Bottle	122
I Cross My Heart	Pure Country	130
(Everything I Do) I Do It for You	Robin Hood: Prince of Thieves	126
I Don't Want to Miss a Thing	Armageddon	135
I Say a Little Prayer	My Best Friend's Wedding	142
I Will Always Love You	The Bodyguard	148
I Will Remember You	The Brothers McMullen	156
Kiss From a Rose	Batman Forever	160
Kissing You	Romeo + Juliet	166
Lane's Theme	8 Seconds	170
Live and Let Die	Live and Let Die	174
Love Story (Where Do I Begin)	Love Story	153
Main Title From "The Fugitive"	The Fugitive	178
Misty	Play Misty for Me	181
Music of My Heart	Music of the Heart	184
My Own True Love (Tara Theme)	Gone With the Wind	190

Title	Movie	Page
New York, New York	On the Town	192
Once in a Lifetime	Only You	194
Over My Head	Titan A.E.	200
Over the Rainbow	The Wizard of Oz	206
The Pink Panther	The Pink Panther	210
Raindrops Keep Falling on My Head	Butch Cassidy and the Sundance Kid	212
Remember Me This Way	Casper	216
The Rose	The Rose	222
Run To You	The Bodyguard	226
Secret Agent Man	The Adventures of Rocky and Bullwinkle	232
Secret Garden	Jerry Maguire	240
The Shadow of Your Smile	The Sandpiper	236
Singin' in the Rain	Singin' in the Rain	245
Somewhere My Love (Lara's Theme)	Doctor Zhivago	250
Somewhere Out There	An American Tail	253
Song From M*A*S*H (Suicide Is Painless)	M*A*S*H	258
Star Wars (Main Theme)	Star Wars	260
Still	Dogma	278
Tears in Heaven	Rush	262
Thank You	Kingdom Come	266
That Thing You Do!	That Thing You Do	274
That's What Friends Are For	Night Shift	285
Themes From "Batman Forever"	Batman Forever	300
Theme From Ice Castles (Through the Eyes of Love)	Ice Castles	292
Theme From Inspector Gadget	Inspector Gadget	304
Theme From "Jurassic Park"	Jurassic Park	306
Theme From "Schindler's List"	Schindler's List	298
There You'll Be	Pearl Harbor	310
Tomorrow	Annie	295
Tomorrow Never Dies	Tomorrow Never Dies	315
Uninvited	City of Angels	322
A View to a Kill	A View to a Kill	327
Wild Wild West (Main Title)	Wild Wild West	332
Win	Men of Honor	337
The Wind Beneath My Wings	Beaches	342
You Must Love Me	Evita	349
Yours Forever	The Perfect Storm	352

Ultimate MOVIE SHOWSTOPPERS

Introduction

"You can be grateful my invention is not for sale, for it would undoubtedly ruin you." Frenchman Auguste Lumière gave this glum advice to would-be investors who asked him about the new film projector he and his brother Louis had designed. The brothers called their invention the Cinématographe, from which we get the word *cinema*. On December 28, 1895, they introduced it to the public by holding history's first movie exhibition at a Paris cafe.

Auguste's dim view of the cinema's market potential may have been understandable. The short film he and his brother exhibited on that long-ago December day wasn't very exciting—it simply showed workers leaving their Lyon factory. History, however, would prove his prediction to be very, very wrong. Going to the movies has become one of the most popular and universally enjoyed pastimes in the world. In the U.S. alone, film industry revenues exceeded $27 billion in the year 2000 from box office receipts plus video sales and rentals.

Why do we love movies so much? For starters, they offer us an easy—and very enjoyable—way to break free from our everyday lives and enter a world of unlimited possibilities. When the theater lights go down, our normal cares seem to disappear. Sitting back in our plush seat, we gladly go along for the ride as movies transport us to places we would never otherwise see, introduce us to people we would never otherwise meet, and put us in the middle of adventures we would never otherwise experience.

Yet movies offer much more than a chance to escape. They also act as a familiar road map, ready to be pulled out when the swirl of life around us becomes too confusing. Events unfold at a dizzying pace in the movies: heroes move in and out of danger with the speed of a runaway freight train, and love is lost and found as quickly as a coin turns.

When we watch movies, we develop an emotional shorthand for keeping pace with a film's swift succession of images. At times when real life takes on this rapid-fire quality, we seek to define things in terms of what we have seen on the big screen. *It was just like a movie.* How often have we heard this declaration from someone who has just experienced a fantastic or catastrophic event?

Music and Motion Pictures

People have recognized the special power of moving pictures to transform us, even before the Lumière brothers invented their film projector. In the early 1800s, magic lantern shows in Europe entertained audiences by showing drawings of moving figures in rapid succession to create the illusion of motion.

By the 1890s, a number of inventors had come up with machines for recording and reproducing motion pictures. Among them was Thomas Edison, who led a team that developed the Kinetoscope, a machine that made it possible to view movies by peeping through two goggle-like openings. Like the Lumière brothers, Edison didn't see much of a future in film—he didn't even bother taking out a European patent for his invention. In his mind, the Kinetoscope was merely a sideline to another of his creations—the phonograph.

Edison was also wrong about the market potential of the cinema, but he certainly got one thing right—movies and music make a great team. In the early twentieth century, the serious filmmakers who began elevating the artistic standards of the new medium realized that music was essential to helping a movie reach its full dramatic power.

Before Warner Bros. ushered in the era of the talkie with *The Jazz Singer* in 1927, the works of these early filmmakers were called silent movies because they had no pre-recorded sound. This was somewhat misleading. As every classic film fan knows, these movies were not really silent since theaters hired organists—and, in bigger houses, entire orchestras—to provide live musical accompaniment to the action on the screen.

The marriage of movies and music has been going strong ever since—and our culture, as well as our lives, has been richer for it.

Love and Music

Romance occupies an exalted place in movies, just as it does in music. So it is not surprising that many of our most popular love songs came from the world of film. Music, with its unique ability to touch our hearts and tug at our memories, adds an achingly sweet quality to movie romances. After all, isn't it really the crescendo of a passionate theme song that first makes us weep when we watch a tearjerker about star-crossed lovers?

By the same token, the lush visual power of film can also imbue any love song with deeper feelings and more fiery passions. Bruce Springsteen's emotive "Secret Garden" glows even more warmly when we think of the first time we heard it, watching Tom Cruise and Renée Zellweger begin their beautifully transforming romance in *Jerry Maguire*.

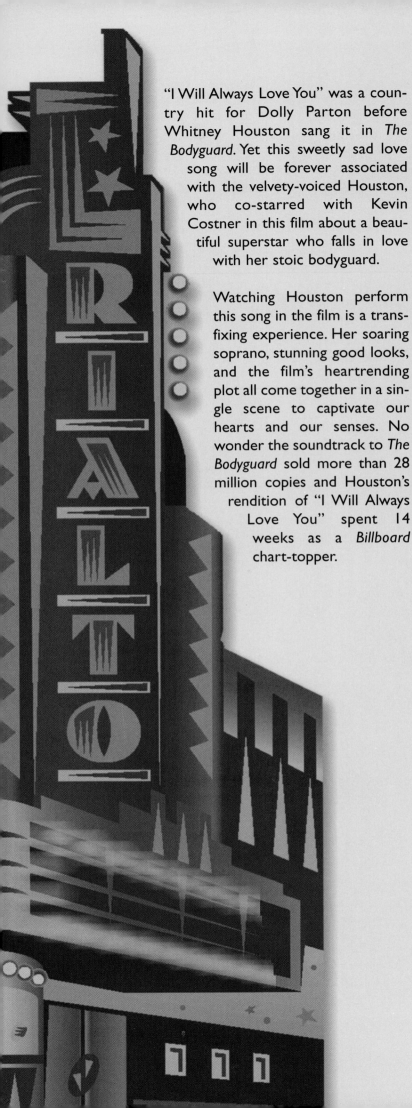

"I Will Always Love You" was a country hit for Dolly Parton before Whitney Houston sang it in *The Bodyguard*. Yet this sweetly sad love song will be forever associated with the velvety-voiced Houston, who co-starred with Kevin Costner in this film about a beautiful superstar who falls in love with her stoic bodyguard.

Watching Houston perform this song in the film is a transfixing experience. Her soaring soprano, stunning good looks, and the film's heartrending plot all come together in a single scene to captivate our hearts and our senses. No wonder the soundtrack to *The Bodyguard* sold more than 28 million copies and Houston's rendition of "I Will Always Love You" spent 14 weeks as a *Billboard* chart-topper.

In some movies, the romantic elements of a song are accentuated further by having the two lovers perform a duet. Beautiful Nicole Kidman and handsome Ewan McGregor lit up the screen as Satine and Christian in the film *Moulin Rouge,* especially in the magical scene when they sing "Come What May." The two lovers begin their duet at a window ledge; then as the camera pulls away, the song and the breathtaking scenery take us on a journey that leaves us in awe of love's power to remake people and places.

Love often has a vaguely poignant quality in movies—and in life. It brings with it a delicate sense of fleetingness and fragility balanced against a strong feeling of having found our true place in this world. We are never so secure, or so vulnerable, as when we are in love. This feeling is at the heart of *Message in a Bottle,* a touching and powerful love story starring Robin Wright Penn as Theresa and Kevin Costner as Garret.

After finding Garret's love letter to his late wife washed on shore in a bottle, Theresa tracks him down. The two fall in love, but fate soon takes Garret away. Theresa is heartbroken, but deep within her soul, she knows that her life is so much richer for the brief love they shared. Theresa's feelings are reflected in the film's beautiful soundtrack, most notably Edwin McCain's love song "I Could Not Ask for More."

Music Sets the Mood

When movies are more about fast action than touching love, music—the universal language—is there to set the mood. In many cases, music seems to act as a turbocharger, revving up the already fast-paced action on the screen. This was clearly the case with "Born to Be Wild," the theme song for the quintessential road movie *Easy Rider,* starring Dennis Hopper as Billy and Peter Fonda as Wyatt.

Who can forget hearing the raw, earthy power of Steppenwolf performing this rebellious anthem at the beginning of the film? Listening to Steppenwolf, we could feel the wind in our hair and the "heavy metal thunder" of the motorcycles. This theme song not only brought us into the movie, but it also made us part of the journey. "Born to Be Wild" connected with '60s youths in ways that went beyond its association with this cult-classic film, which helped the song reach a No. 2 *Billboard* chart position.

Few songs have set the mood for action films with the verve and flair of John Barry's compositions for many of the most famous James Bond movies. Barry's classic theme song for *Goldfinger,* performed by the charismatic Shirley Bassey, became one of the most recognizable movie themes of the '60s, reaching a No. 8 *Billboard* chart position in 1965.

Just as music can send a current of nail-biting excitement through an action drama, it can also create a soothing mood for a more introspective movie. Soft melodies and heartfelt theme songs often focus our attention on the inner lives of the characters on the screen, giving us a greater appreciation of their hopes and dreams, which often turn out to be so much like those we harbor in our own hearts.

Such songs tend to be forever interwoven with our most cherished movie memories. Listening to these songs brings the movies of our past back to life, infusing almost-forgotten images with the color and vitality that so beguiled us when we first encountered them all those years ago at our hometown theater.

Among the most evocative movie songs of all time is "Somewhere Over the Rainbow," by Harold Arlen and E.Y. Harburg. Judy Garland, who played Dorothy in the 1939 classic *The Wizard of Oz* and performed this song for the movie, won an Oscar for her outstanding performance as a "screen juvenile."

Generations of great performers have come and gone since the teenage Garland performed this movie song, yet the years have not diminished its haunting beauty. Listening to Garland, we cannot help but be filled with a sense of hope and yearning, knowing that however lost we might sometimes feel, there is always the promise of a brighter tomorrow out there "over the rainbow."

Giving us a glimpse of this special place is part of the magic of movies—and of music.

Music Trivia

1. The earliest films simply chronicled everyday events, such as a train arriving at a station, rather than told stories. They usually were less than ten minutes in length.

2. *The Great Train Robbery,* a western filmed in New Jersey in 1903, was among the first films to use editing and other narrative techniques. It ushered in a new era in filmmaking.

3. Until around 1913, the film industry was headquartered in New York, not Hollywood. The movie actors themselves were virtually unknown because they received no billing in the film's credits.

4. In 1902, a Los Angeles shop became the first business dedicated exclusively to showing movies to the public. The first true movie theater opened in Pittsburgh in 1905. It charged a nickel for admission, which led to the name *nickelodeon.* By 1907, there were more than 3,000 nickelodeons across the U.S., and daily attendance was about two million.

5. The first film festival was held in Venice, Italy, in 1932.

6. The Oscar statue presented to Academy Award-winners stands 13.5 inches tall and weighs 8.5 pounds.

7. For a film to be eligible for an Academy Award, it must be exhibited for paid admission at a commercial movie theater in the Los Angeles area for at least one week between January 1 and midnight December 31 of that year.

8. In 1939, Hattie McDaniel became the first African-American to win an Academy Award for her role in *Gone With the Wind.*

9. *Doctor Zhivago,* a movie centered around the Russian Revolution, was filmed in Spain.

10. Italians have won ten Academy Awards for Best Foreign Film, more than moviemakers from any other country.

11. The Academy Awards for Best Actor and Best Actress went to stars from the same motion picture twice in the 1990s: Anthony Hopkins and Jodi Foster won for *Silence of the Lambs,* and Jack Nicholson and Helen Hunt won for *As Good as It Gets.* This happened only once in the 1980s.

12. In 2000, *Gladiator* became the second film set in the ancient Roman Empire to win an Academy Award for Best Picture. *Ben-Hur* earned this honor in 1959, five years before *Gladiator* star Russell Crowe was born.

AMERICAN PIE

Words and Music by
DON McLEAN

Slowly and freely ♩ = 72

Prologue:

A long, long time a-go,___ I can still re-mem-ber how that mu-sic used to make___ me smile.___ And I knew that if___ I had my chance, I could make___ those peo-ple dance___ and may-be, they'd___ be hap-py for a while.

American Pie - 7 - 1

Moderately fast ♩ = 124

Verse 2:
I met a girl who sang the blues
And I asked her for some happy news,
But she just smiled and turned away.
I went down to the sacred store,
Where I heard the music years before,
But the man there said the music wouldn't play.
And in the streets, the children screamed,
The lovers cried and the poets dreamed.
But not a word was spoken;
The church bells were all broken.
And the three men I admire most,
The Father, Son, and Holy Ghost,
They caught the last train for the coast
The day the music died.
And they were singin':
(To Chorus:)

From the Original Motion Picture Soundtrack "THE THREE MUSKETEERS"

ALL FOR LOVE

Written by
BRYAN ADAMS, ROBERT JOHN "MUTT" LANGE
and MICHAEL KAMEN

All for Love - 6 - 1

18

All for Love - 6 - 4

From the Motion Picture AUSTIN POWERS: The Spy Who Shagged Me

BEAUTIFUL STRANGER

Words and Music by
MADONNA CICCONE and WILLIAM ORBIT

1. Have-n't we met?

You're some kind of beau-ti-ful strang-er.

You could be good

Beautiful Stranger - 7 - 1

BECAUSE YOU LOVED ME
(Theme from "Up Close & Personal")

Words and Music by
DIANE WARREN

Slowly ♩ = 76

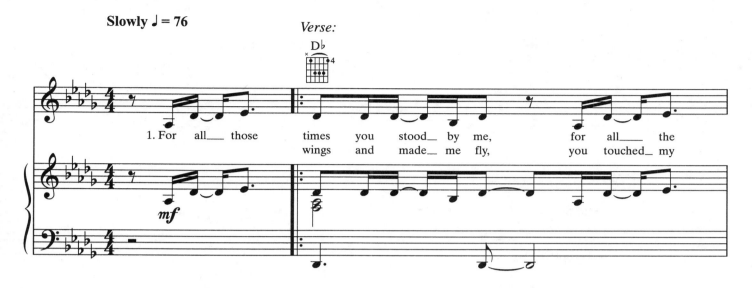

1. For all those times you stood by me, for all the
wings and made me fly, you touched my

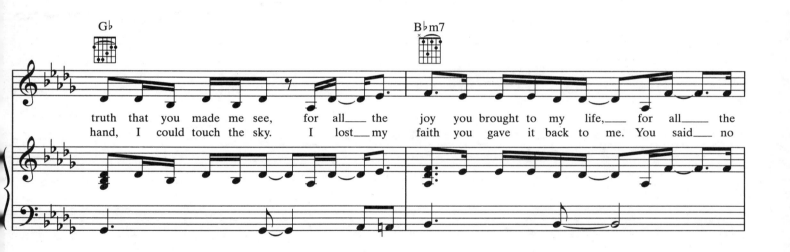

truth that you made me see, for all the joy you brought to my life, for all the
hand, I could touch the sky. I lost my faith you gave it back to me. You said no

wrong that you made right, for ev-ery dream you made come true, for all the
star was out of reach, you stood by me and I stood tall. I had your

Because You Loved Me - 5 - 1

Music from the Original Motion Picture SHREK

BEST YEARS OF OUR LIVES

By
DAVID JAYMES and GEOFFREY DEANE

Best Years of Our Lives - 7 - 1

D.S. % al Coda

Coda

best years of our lives. *See, you always considered me like an ugly donkey,*

and treat me like a Nostradamus is why I had to get my shine on. I bring a little somethin'

to keep my mind on, 'cause you had my mind gone. *Uh uh, uh uh, uh hey, turn the lights on.*

Verse 2:
When we first met, I could hardly believe
The things that would happen and we could achieve.
So, let's stay together for all of our time.
And girl, I'm so thankful that you are still mine.
(To Chorus:)

Verse 3:
My world's a better place 'cause I know you're mine.
This love is so real and it's no surprise.
C'mon and say, yeah, I gotta show you.
Because through the years, I'll be right by your side.
(To Chorus:)

BORN TO BE WILD

Words and Music by
MARS BONFIRE

Born to Be Wild - 3 - 1

42

Born to Be Wild - 3 - 2

CAN'T FIGHT THE MOONLIGHT
(Theme from Coyote Ugly)

Words and Music by
DIANE WARREN

Moderately slow ♩ = 98

Verse:

1. Un - der a lov - er's sky, gon - na be with you, and no
2. There's no es - cape from love. Once the gen - tle breeze weaves

one's gon - na be a - round. If you think that you won't fall, we'll just wait
its spell up - on your heart, no mat - ter what you think, it won't be

Bridge:

48

Chorus:

to re - sist,___ try to hide___ from my kiss,___ but you know,___ but you know___ that you

can't fight the moon - light. Deep___ in the dark,___ you'll sur - ren - der your heart.___ Don't you know,___

___ don't you know___ that you can't fight the moon - light, no,_____ you can't fight

it. You can try___ it. It's gon-na get to your heart.___

From the 20th Century-Fox Motion Picture "A CERTAIN SMILE"

A CERTAIN SMILE

Words by
PAUL FRANCIS WEBSTER

Music by
SAMMY FAIN

Moderately slow

A Certain Smile - 3 - 1

From the Twentieth Century Fox Motion Picture MOULIN ROUGE

COME WHAT MAY

Words and Music by
DAVID BAERWALD

Come What May - 7 - 1

Verse 1:

(He:) 1. Nev-er knew I could feel like this, like I've___ nev-er seen___ the sky___ ___ be-fore. Want to van-ish in-side your kiss. Ev-'ry day___ I love you more and___ more. Lis-ten to___ my heart.___ Can you hear it sing, tell-ing me___ to give___ you ev-'ry-thing.

Chorus:

Bridge:

DIAMONDS ARE FOREVER

Moderately (♩ = 104)

Lyric by DON BLACK
Music by JOHN BARRY

Dia-monds are for - ev - er,_____ they are all I need to please me,_____

_____ they can stim - u - late and tease me,_____ they won't

leave in the night, I've no fear that they might de - sert me._____

Diamonds Are Forever - 3 - 1

CHANGE THE WORLD

Words and Music by
TOMMY SIMS, GORDON KENNEDY
and WAYNE KIRKPATRICK

Music From and Inspired By the Motion Picture POKÉMON - THE FIRST MOVIE

DON'T SAY YOU LOVE ME

Moderately slow ♩ = 100

Verse 1:

Words and Music by
MARION RAVN, MARIT LARSEN,
PETER ZIZZO and JIMMY BRALOWER

1. Got in-tro-duced to you by a friend.___

You were cute and all that. Ba-by, you set the trend,___ yes, you did,___ oh. The next thing I know, we're down at the

cin-e-ma. We're sit-tin' there, you said you loved me.___ What's that___ a-bout?

Don't Say You Love Me - 6 - 1

Verses 2 & 3:

2. You're mov-ing too fast, I don't un-der-stand you.
3. Here's how I play,____ here's where you stand.____

I'm not read-y yet. Ba-by, I can't pre-tend,____ no, I can't.____
Here's what to prove to get an-y fur-ther than____ where it's been.____

The best I can do is tell you to talk to me.____ It's pos-si-ble,____ e-
I'll make it clear; not gon-na tell you twice.____ Take it slow, you keep

ven-tu-al.____ Love will find____ a way. (Love will find____ a way.____)
push-ing me. You're push-ing me____ a-way. (Push-ing me____ a-way.____)

70

Chorus:

ENDLESS LOVE

Words and Music
LIONEL RICHIE

A FOOL IN LOVE

Words and Music by
RANDY NEWMAN

A Fool in Love - 5 - 1

F♯
D13
love.
G
Gmaj7
G(9)
G
Gmaj7
2. When you're a fool in love,___ seems like the skies are
D7
Am7
D7
al - ways gray. You turn a - round to some-one in your way, and it's
G
you, and___ you're in love.

From the Twentieth Century Fox Motion Picture "ONE FINE DAY"

FOR THE FIRST TIME

Words and Music by
JAMES NEWTON HOWARD,
ALLAN RICH and JUD FRIEDMAN

Slowly ♩ = 62

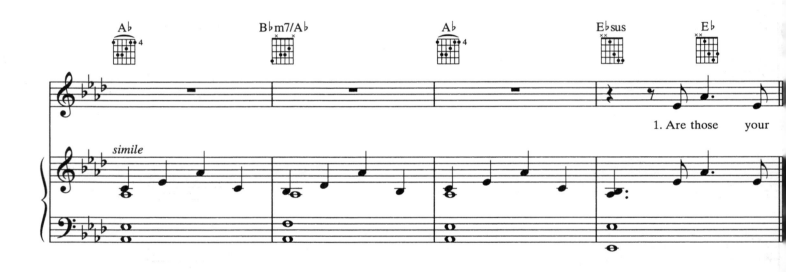

(with pedal)

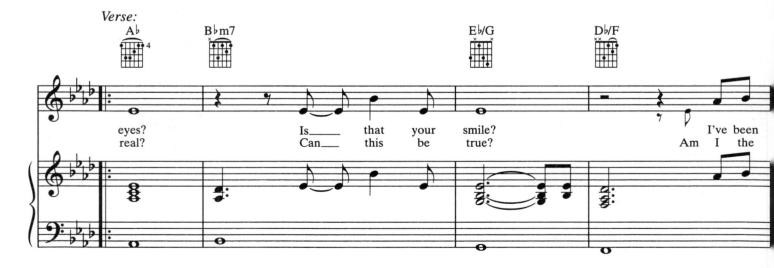

1. Are those your

Verse:

eyes?
real?
Is___ that your smile?
Can___ this be true?
I've been
Am I the

For the First Time - 6 - 1

Now I un - der - stand____ what_____ love___ is,

love___ is for the first time.____

FOR YOU I WILL

Words and Music by
DIANE WARREN

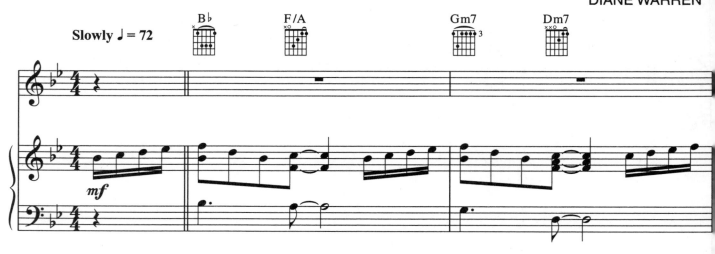

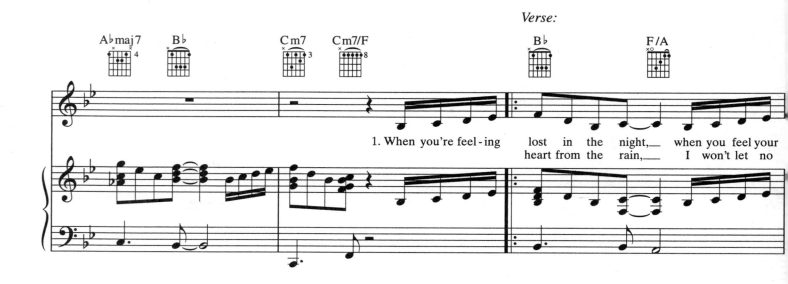

Verse:

1. When you're feel-ing lost in the night,___ when you feel your
heart from the rain,___ I won't let no

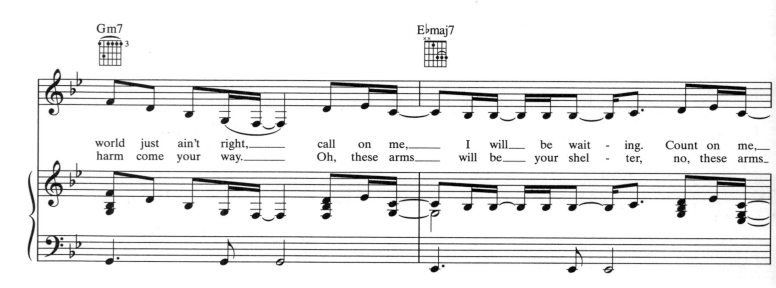

world just ain't right,_____ call on me,_____ I will___ be wait-ing. Count on me,
harm come your way._____ Oh, these arms___ will be___ your shel-ter, no, these arms_

I will be there. Any time the times get too tough, any time your
won't let you down. If there is a mountain to move, I will move that

best ain't enough, I'll be the one to make it better.
mountain for you. I'm here for you, I'm here forever.

I'll be there to protect you, see you through.
I will be a fortress, tall and strong. I'll

I'll be there, and there is nothing I won't do.
keep you safe, I'll stand beside you, right or wrong. I will cross the

Chorus:

GOLDFINGER

Lyric by LESLIE BRICUSSE
and ANTHONY NEWLEY
Music by JOHN BARRY

* Original recording in E.

Goldfinger - 3 - 1

THE GREATEST LOVE OF ALL

Words by
LINDA CREED

Music by
MICHAEL MASSER

The Greatest Love of All - 4 - 1

The Greatest Love of All - 4 - 2

98

The Greatest Love of All - 4 - 3

The Greatest Love of All - 4 - 4

THE GREEN MILE
(End Title)

Composed by
THOMAS NEWMAN

The Green Mile - 4 - 1

The Green Mile - 4 - 2

From the Original Motion Picture Soundtrack "DON JUAN DeMARCO"

HAVE YOU EVER REALLY LOVED A WOMAN?

Lyrics by
BRYAN ADAMS and
ROBERT JOHN "MUTT" LANGE

Music by
MICHAEL KAMEN

Have You Ever Really Loved a Woman? - 6 - 1

107

She will be there for you, tak-ing good care___ of you.___ You real-ly got-ta *love___your wom-an.___*

(Instrumental solo . . .

. . . end solo)

And when you

find your-self ly - ing help - less in___ her arms,_____ you know you real - ly

Have You Ever Really Loved a Woman? - 6 - 4

From the Touchstone Motion Picture "CON AIR"

HOW DO I LIVE

Words and Music by
DIANE WARREN

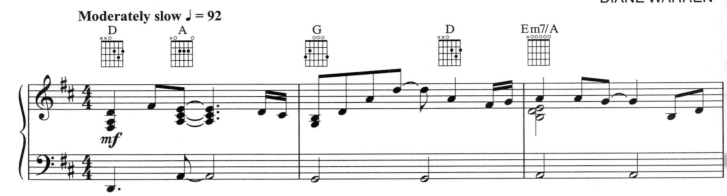

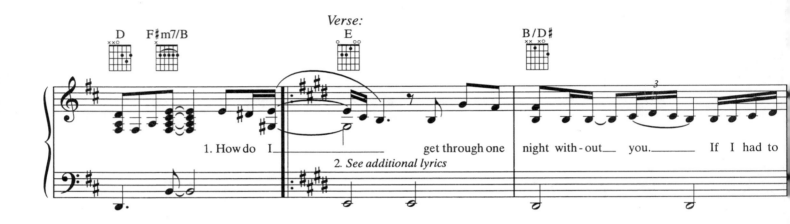

How Do I Live - 4 - 1

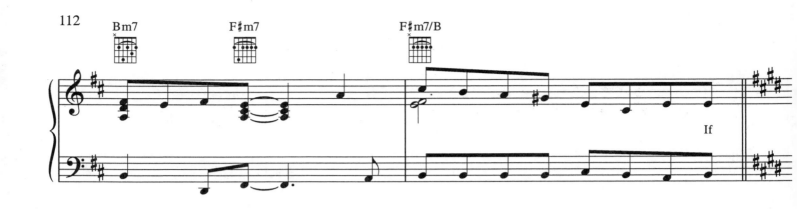

If

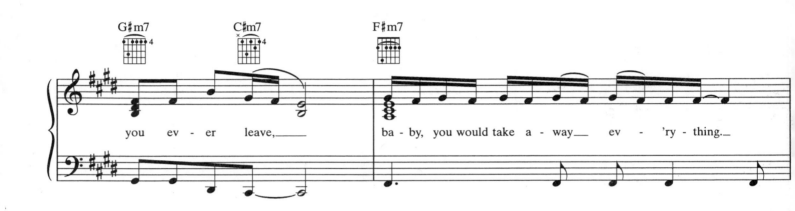

you ev - er leave,_____ ba - by, you would take a - way___ ev - 'ry - thing._

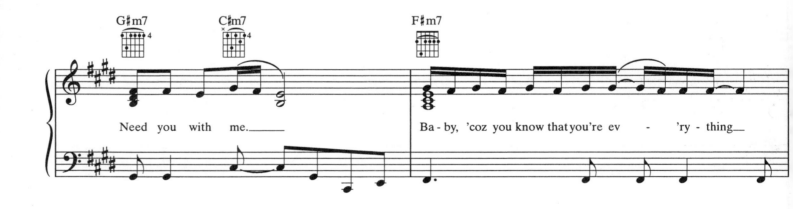

Need you with me._____ Ba - by, 'coz you know that you're ev - 'ry - thing___

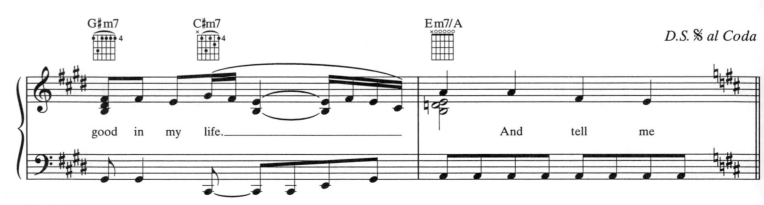

D.S. % al Coda

good in my life._____ And tell me

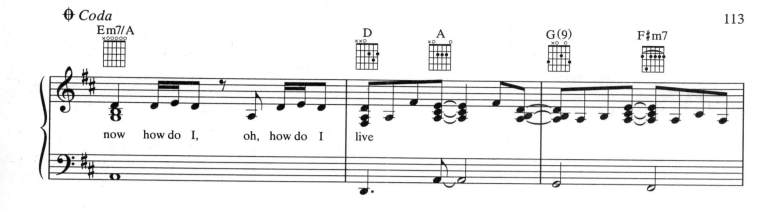

now   how do I,   oh, how do I   live

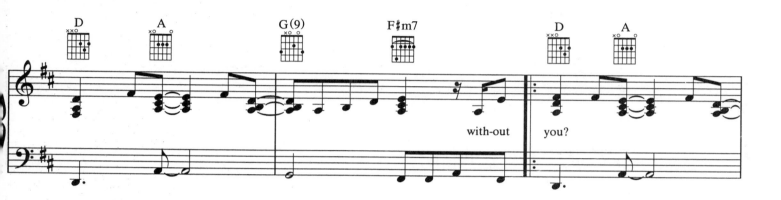

with-out   you?

Repeat ad lib. and fade
(vocal 1st time only)

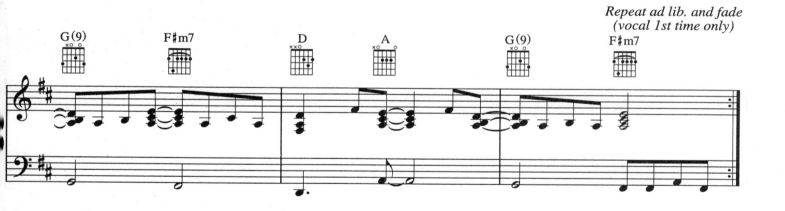

Verse 2:
Without you, there'd be no sun in my sky,
There would be no love in my life,
There'd be no world left for me.
And I, baby, I don't know what I would do,
I'd be lost if I lost you.
If you ever leave,
Baby, you would take away everything real in my life.
And tell me now...
(To Chorus:)

I BELIEVE I CAN FLY

Words and Music by
R. KELLY

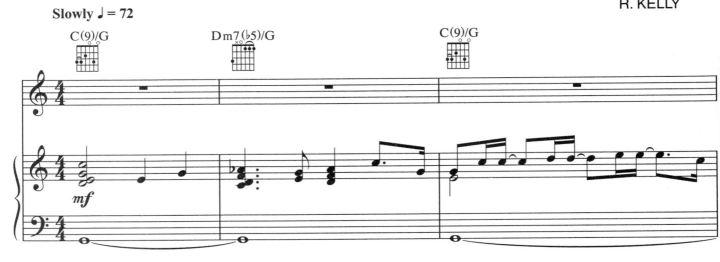

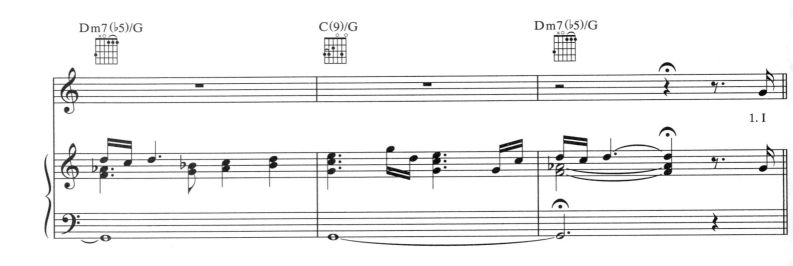

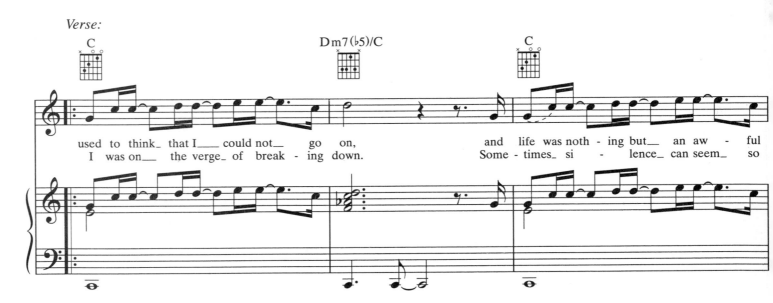

Verse:

used to think_ that I___ could not_ go on,
I was on___ the verge_ of break - ing down.
Some - times_ si - lence_ can seem_ so

I Believe I Can Fly - 5 - 1

I CAN SEE CLEARLY NOW

Words and Music by
JOHNNY NASH

I Can See Clearly Now - 3 - 1

Verse 3:
I can see clearly now, the rain is gone.
I can see all obstacles in my way.
Here is that rainbow I've been praying for,
It's gonna be a bright, bright sunshiny day.
It's gonna be a bright, bright sunshiny day.

I COULD NOT ASK FOR MORE

Words and Music by
DIANE WARREN

I Could Not Ask for More - 4 - 1

Chorus:

more_ than this time to-geth - er. I could not ask for more than this time with you.___ Ev-'ry

prayer I have's_ been an-swered and ev-'ry dream I have's_come true.___ And

right here in this mo-ment is right where I'm meant to be._ Oh, here with_ you, here with_

me,_____ oh._____

From the Motion Picture "Robin Hood: Prince of Thieves"

(EVERYTHING I DO) I DO IT FOR YOU

Written by
BRYAN ADAMS, ROBERT JOHN LANGE
and MICHAEL KAMEN

(Everything I Do) I Do It for You - 4 - 1

129

(Everything I Do) I Do It for You - 4 - 4

I CROSS MY HEART

Words and Music by
STEVE DORFF and ERIC KAZ

Our love is un-con-di-tion-al,___
(See additional lyrics)

we knew it from the start.___ I see it in your eyes,___

___ you can feel it from___ my___ heart.___

132

I Cross My Heart - 5 - 3

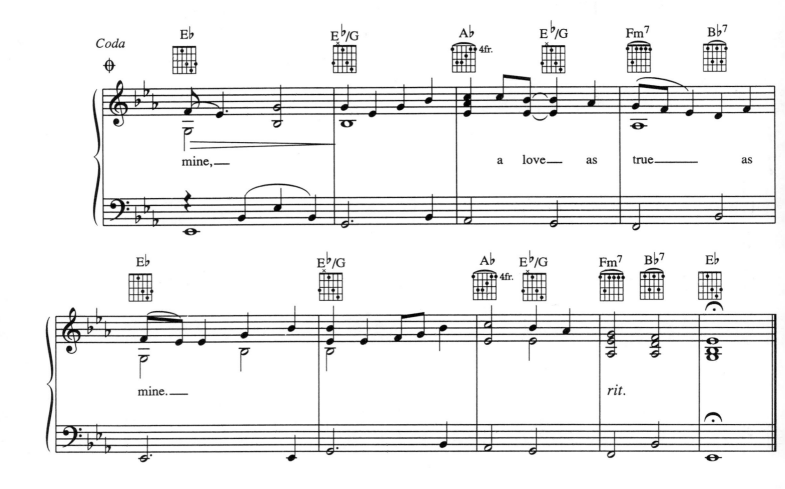

Coda

mine,— a love— as true— as

mine.— *rit.*

Additional Lyrics

2. You will always be the miracle
   That makes my life complete.
   And as long as there's a breath in me
   I'll make yours just as sweet.
   As we look into the future,
   It's as far as we can see.
   So let's make each tomorrow
   Be the best that it can be.
   (To Chorus)

From Touchstone Pictures' ARMAGEDDON

I DON'T WANT TO MISS A THING

Words and Music by
DIANE WARREN

Don't Want to Miss a Thing - 7 - 1

From "MY BEST FRIEND'S WEDDING"

I SAY A LITTLE PRAYER

Words by
HAL DAVID

Music by
BURT BACHARACH

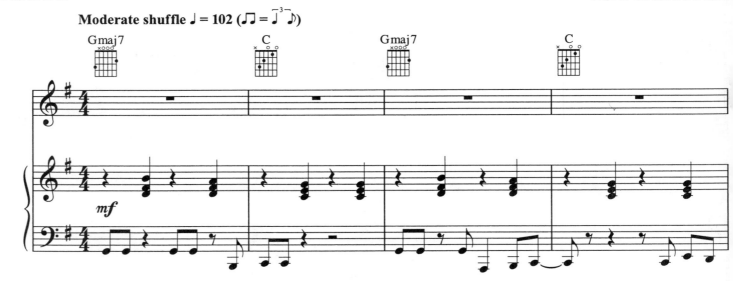

I Say a Little Prayer - 6 - 1

Say a Little Prayer - 6 - 2

Chorus:

146

Chorus:

I Say a Little Prayer - 6 - 6

I WILL ALWAYS LOVE YOU

Words and Music by
DOLLY PARTON

I Will Always Love You - 5 - 1

150

I Will Always Love You - 5 - 3

Verse 3: Instrumental solo

Verse 4:
I hope life treats you kind
And I hope you have all you've dreamed of.
And I wish to you, joy and happiness.
But above all this, I wish you love.
(To Chorus:)

From the Motion Picture "LOVE STORY"

LOVE STORY (Where Do I Begin)

Lyric by
CARL SIGMAN

FRAN...

Where Do I Be-gin _____ to tell the sto-ry of how great a love can be, _____

With her first hel-lo _____ she gave a mean-ing to this emp-ty world of mine; _____

_____ The sweet love sto-ry that is old-er than the sea, The sim-ple truth a-bout the

_____ There'd nev-er be an-oth-er love, an-oth-er time; She came in-to my life and

love she brings to me? _____ Where do I start? _____

made the liv-ing fine. _____

Love Story (Where Do I Begin) - 3 - 1

From the Fox Searchlight Film "THE BROTHERS McMULLEN"

I WILL REMEMBER YOU

Words and Music by
SARAH McLACHLAN, SEAMUS EGAN
and DAVE MERENDA

I Will Remember You - 4 - 1

Verse 2:
So afraid to love you,
More afraid to lose.
I'm clinging to a past
That doesn't let me choose.
Where once there was a darkness,
A deep and endless night,
You gave me everything you had,
Oh, you gave me life.
(To Chorus:)

(Optional Verse 1 — Album version)
Remember the good times that we had,
I let them slip away from us when things got bad.
Now clearly I first saw you smiling in the sun.
I wanna feel your warmth upon me,
I wanna be the one.
(To Chorus:)

KISS FROM A ROSE

Words and Music by
SEAL

162

tell you, so much he can say.___ You re-main my pow-er, my plea-sure my

pain. To me you're like a growing ad - dic - tion that I can't de -

ny. Now won't you tell me, is that health-y, ba - by? But did you know that when it snows, my

D.S. 𝄋 al Chorus and fade

eyes be-come large and the light that you shine can't be seen? Ba -

KISSING YOU
(Love Theme From "ROMEO + JULIET")

Words and Music by
DES'REE and TIM ATACK

Moderately slow ♩. = 112

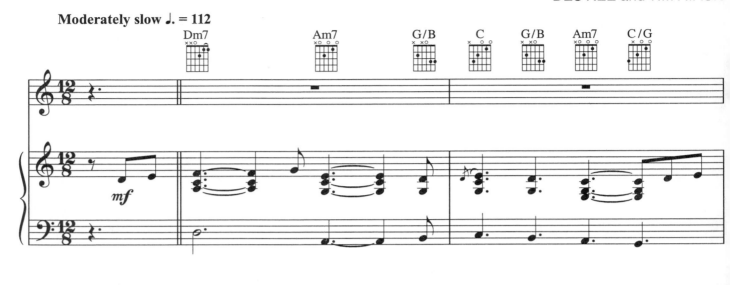

Verse 1:

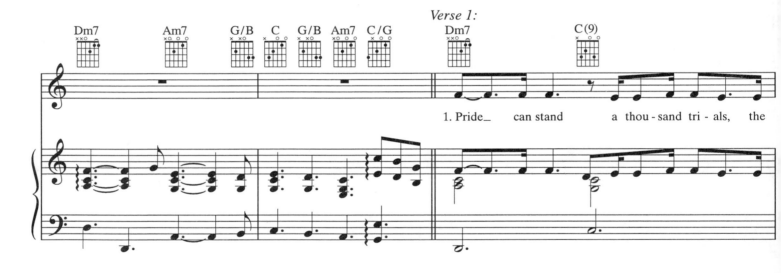

1. Pride_ can stand a thou-sand tri - als, the

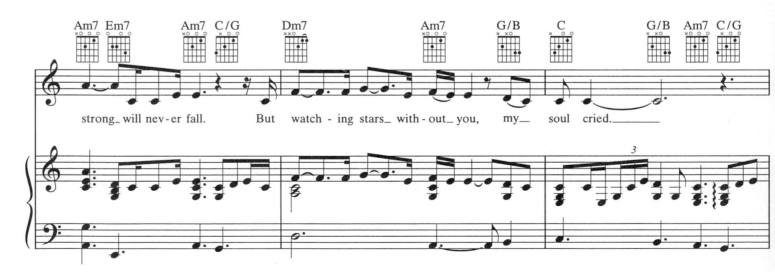

strong_ will nev-er fall. But watch-ing stars_ with-out_ you, my_ soul cried._____

Kissing You - 4 - 1

From the Original Motion Picture Soundtrack "8 SECONDS"

LANE'S THEME

Composed by
BILL CONTI

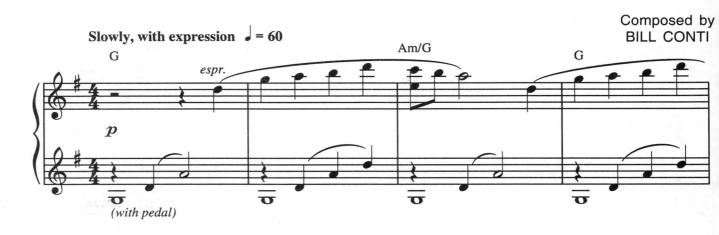

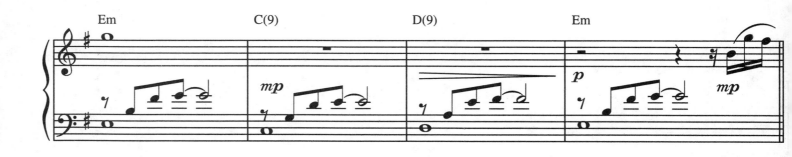

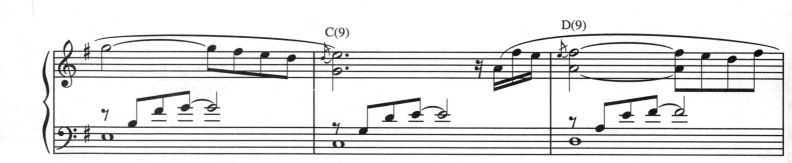

Lane's Theme - 4 - 1

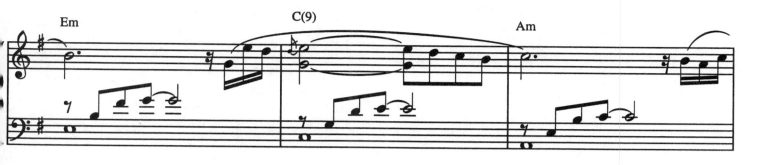

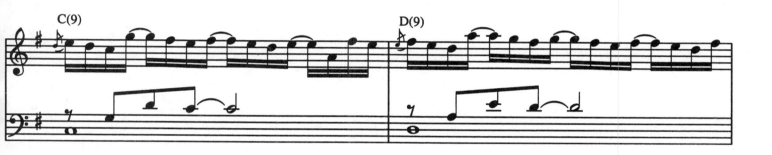

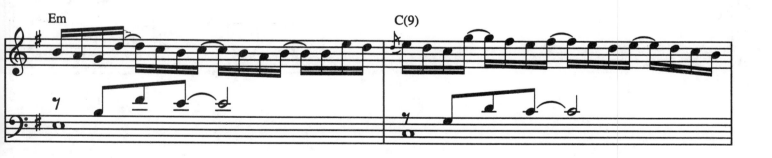

Lane's Theme - 4 - 2

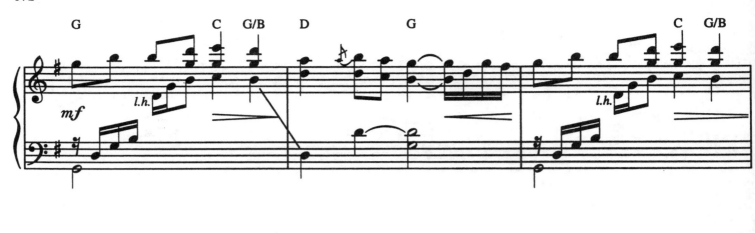

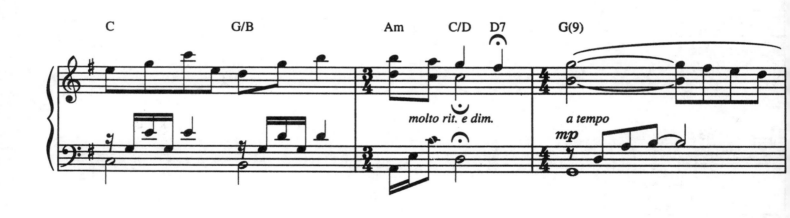

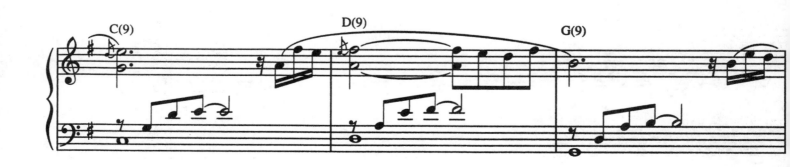

Lane's Theme - 4 - 4

From the United Artists Motion Picture "LIVE AND LET DIE"

LIVE AND LET DIE

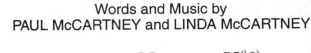

Words and Music by
PAUL McCARTNEY and LINDA McCARTNEY

Live and Let Die - 4 - 1

give the oth - er fel - low hell!____

D.C. al Coda

Coda

MAIN TITLE FROM "THE FUGITIVE"

Music by
JAMES NEWTON HOWARD

Main Title From "The Fugitive" - 3 - 1

180

MISTY

Words by JOHNNY BURKE

Music by ERROLL GARNER

Slowly, with expression

Refrain

Look at me, I'm as help-less as a kit-ten up a tree, and I feel like I'm cling-ing to a cloud; I can't_____ un-der-stand,_____ I get mist-y just hold-ing your hand._____ Walk my

Misty - 3 - 1

From the Miramax Motion Picture "Music Of The Heart"

MUSIC OF MY HEART

Words and Music by
DIANE WARREN

1. You'll nev-er know_____ what you've
2. You were the one_____ al-ways

done for me,___ what your faith in me___ has
on my side,___ al-ways stand-ing by,___

Music of My Heart - 6 - 1

MY OWN TRUE LOVE
Based on "Tara Theme"

Words by
MACK DAVID

Music by
MAX STEINER

My Own True Love - 2 - 1

NEW YORK, NEW YORK

Words by
BETTY COMDEN and ADOLPH GREEN

Music by
LEONARD BERNSTEIN

ONCE IN A LIFETIME

Words and Music by
WALTER AFANASIEFF, MICHAEL BOLTON
and DIANE WARREN

1. Some peo-ple fill_ their lives_ with emp - ty nights_ and days_ that slip a - way.
2. Some peo-ple live_ their lives_ in com - pro - mise and hide_ their dreams a - way.

198

From the Twentieth Century Fox Motion Picture TITAN A. E.

OVER MY HEAD

Words and Music by
JEREMY A. POPOFF

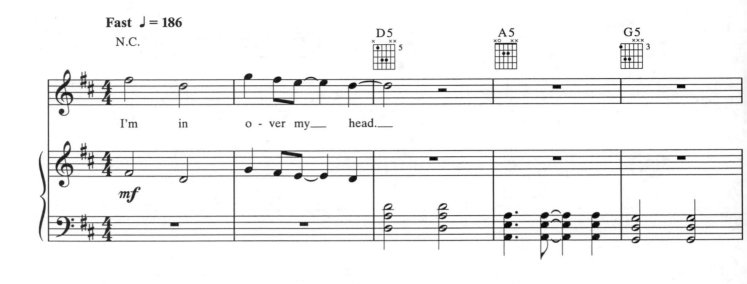

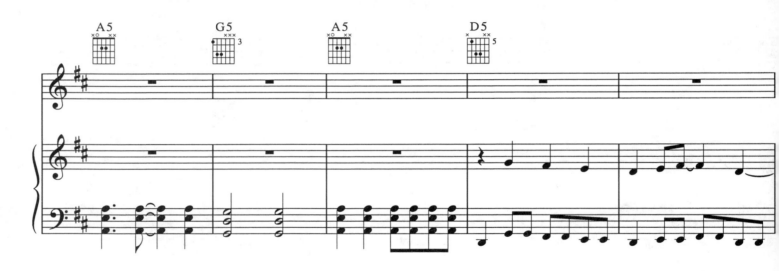

Over My Head - 6 - 1

202

OVER THE RAINBOW

Lyric By
E.Y. HARBURG

Music by
HAROLD ARLEN

Theme Song From the Mirisch-G&E Production "THE PINK PANTHER," A United Artists Release

THE PINK PANTHER

Music by HENRY MANCINI

Moderately Mysterioso

From the 20th Century-Fox Film "BUTCH CASSIDY AND THE SUNDANCE KID"

RAINDROPS KEEP FALLIN' ON MY HEAD

Words by
HAL DAVID

Music by
BURT BACHARACH

Raindrops Keep Fallin' on My Head - 4 - 1

214

Raindrops Keep Fallin' on My Head - 4 - 3

From the Universal Motion Picture "CASPER"

REMEMBER ME THIS WAY

Lyrics by
LINDA THOMPSON

Music by
DAVID FOSTER

From the Twentieth Century-Fox Motion Picture "THE ROSE"

THE ROSE

Words and Music by
AMANDA McBROOM

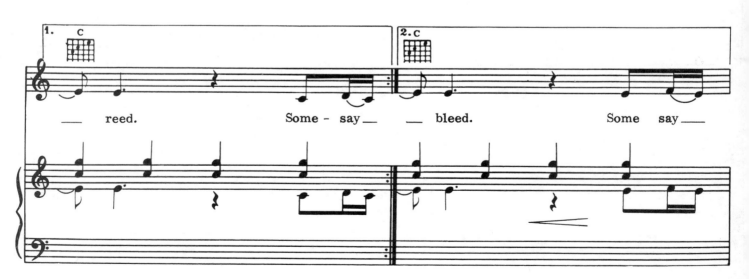

The Rose - 4 - 1

soul a - fraid of dy - in' that nev - er _____ learns to
seed that with the sun's ___ love in the

live. _____ When the ___

spring be - comes the rose.

play 3 times

From the Motion Picture "THE BODYGUARD"

RUN TO YOU

Words and Music by
JUD FRIEDMAN and ALLAN RICH

From the Universal Motion Picture "The Adventures of Rocky and Bullwinkle"

SECRET AGENT MAN

Words and Music by
P.F. SLOAN and STEVE BAR

Secret Agent Man - 4 - 1

ber   and ta - ken 'way__ your   name.__

2. Be -

From the 20th Century-Fox Motion Picture "THE SANDPIPER"

THE SHADOW OF YOUR SMILE

(Love Theme From "The Sandpiper")

Lyrics by
PAUL FRANCIS WEBSTER

Music by
JOHNNY MANDEL

The Shadow of Your Smile - 4 - 1

The Shadow of Your Smile - 4 - 4

SECRET GARDEN

Words and Music by
BRUCE SPRINGSTEEN

Moderately

Verse:

1. She'll let you in her house___ if you come knock-in' late at night.
2.3. *See additional lyrics*

se - cret gar - den where ev - 'ry - thing you want,___

where ev - 'ry - thing you need___

will al - ways stay___

a mil - lion miles___ a -

way. *(1st time only)*

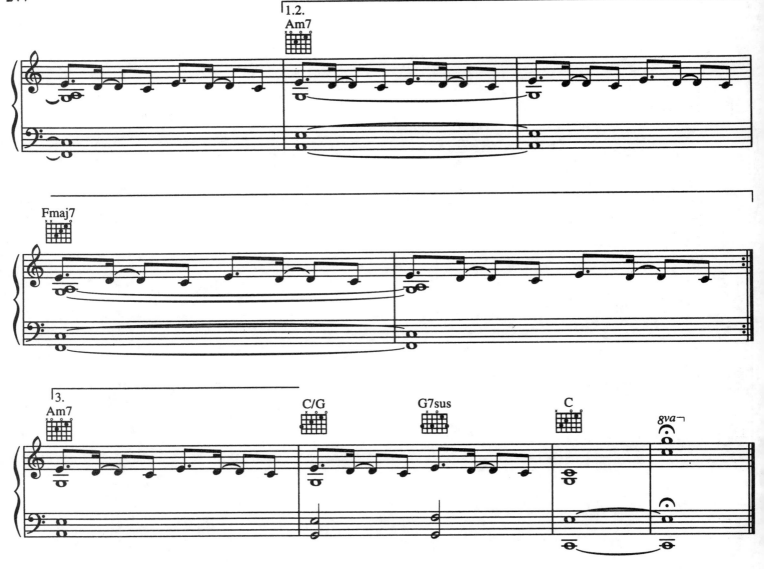

Verse 2:
She'll let you in her car to go drivin' 'round.
She'll let you into the parts of herself
That'll bring you down.
She'll let you in her heart if you got a hammer and a vise.
But into her secret garden, don't think twice.
(To Bridge:)

Verse 3:
She'll lead you down a path,
There'll be tenderness in the air.
She'll let you come just far enough
So you know she's really there.
She'll look at you and smile and her eyes will say
She's got a secret garden
Where everything you want,
Where everything you need
Will always stay a million miles away.

From the Metro-Goldwyn-Mayer Musical Production "SINGIN' IN THE RAIN"

SINGIN' IN THE RAIN

Lyric by
ARTHUR FREED

Music by
NACIO HERB BROWN

I'm sing - in' in the rain, just sing - in' in the

Singin' in the Rain - 5 - 1

METRO-GOLDWYN-MAYER presents DAVID LEAN'S FILM "DOCTOR ZHIVAGO"

SOMEWHERE, MY LOVE
(Lara's Theme From "Doctor Zhivago")

Lyric by
PAUL FRANCIS WEBSTER

Music by
MAURICE JARRE

Somewhere, My Love - 3 - 1

SOMEWHERE OUT THERE

Words and Music by
JAMES HORNER, BARRY MANN
and CYNTHIA WEIL

Somewhere out there beneath the pale moonlight someone's thinkin' of me and

Somewhere Out There - 5 - 1

through, then we'll be to- geth - er some-where out there, out

where dreams come true.

*From the Twentieth Century Fox Motion Picture "M*A*S*H"*

SONG FROM "M*A*S*H"
(Suicide Is Painless)

Words and Music by
MIKE ALTMAN and JOHNNY MANDEL

Through ear-ly morn-ing fog __ I see __ vis-ions of __ the things __ to be: __ the pains that are __ with-held __ for me. __ I re-a-lize __ and I __ can see, __ that su-i-cide __ is pain-less, it brings on man-y chang-

1. Try to find a way to make
   All our little joys relate
   Without that ever-present hate
   But now I know that it's too late.
   And, Chorus

3. The game of life is hard to play,
   I'm going to lose it anyway,
   The losing card I'll someday lay,
   So this is all I have to say,
   That: Chorus

4. The only way to win, is cheat
   And lay it down before I'm beat,
   And to another give a seat
   For that's the only painless feat.
   'Cause: Chorus

5. The sword of time will pierce our skins,
   It doesn't hurt when it begins
   But as it works it's way on in,
   The pain grows stronger, watch it grin.
   For: Chorus

6. A brave man once requested me
   To answer questions that are key,
   Is it to be or not to be
   And I replied; "Oh, why ask me."
   'Cause: Chorus

From the Motion Pictures "STAR WARS" and "THE EMPIRE STRIKES BACK"
A Lucasfilm Ltd. Production - A Twentieth Century-Fox Release

STAR WARS
(Main Theme)

Music by JOHN WILLIAMS

March (Majestic)

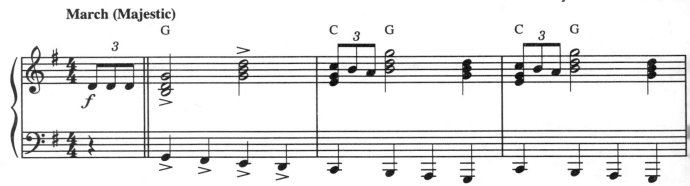

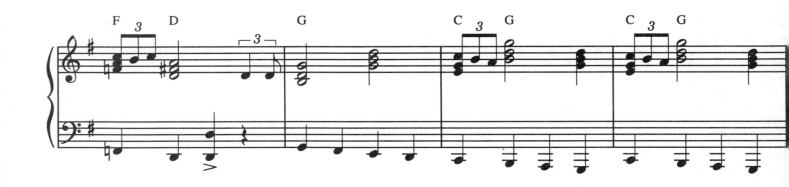

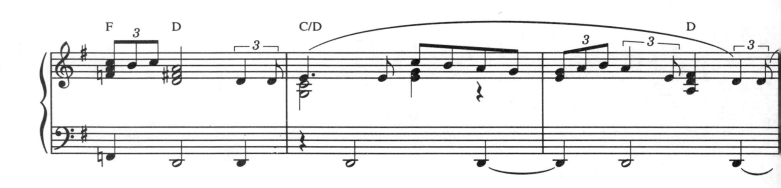

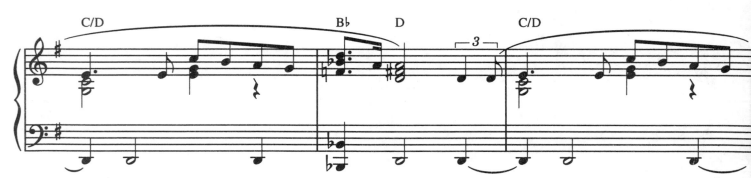

Star Wars (Main Theme) - 2 - 1

Star Wars (Main Theme) - 2 - 2

TEARS IN HEAVEN

Words and Music by
WILL JENNINGS and ERIC CLAPTON

Tears in Heaven - 4 - 1

264

THANK YOU

Words and Music by
KIRK FRANKLIN

Thank You - 8 - 1

me, you gave your life, and now my life, it has new mean-in'. When I

think a-bout your grace, (grace) and I fi-n'lly see your face, (face)

there's one thing I need to say, want to say, yeah:

𝄋 Chorus:

(Thank you, Lord, for lov-ing me; thank you, Lord, for keep-ing me.

Bridge:

D.S. 𝄋 al Coda

Coda

Cm   A♭   G7(♯5)

Thank you for___ that day___ you came___ and broke the chains___ and set___ me free.___

Cm   /B♭ A♭   Fm7   /A♭ B♭

Thank you for___ an-oth-er chance;___ you gave me joy,___ now I___ can dance.___) All my

Fm7   E♭2/G   N.C.

peo-ple o-pen up your mouth___ and let me hear you say thank___ you, (thank___ you.) thank___ you.

Verse 2:
When I was lonely, and I needed someone to hold me,
You were beside me, when my nights got cold and lonely, woah.
You never let me down when no one else could be found.
I always count on you to see me through. I'm telling you, yeah,
You're the reason, Jesus, I'm alive and breathin'.
For me, you gave your life, and now my life, it has new meaning.
Because of your grace, I can see your face.
And when I do, there's just one thing I want to say, gotta say:
(To Chorus:)

From the Twentieth Century Fox Motion Picture

THAT THING YOU DO!

Words and Music by
ADAM SCHLESINGER

1. You_____ know do-in' that thing you do._____ And I'm
2. I_____ know all the games you play._____
3. (Guitar solo ad lib....

Break-in' my heart in-to a mil-lion piec-es
gon-na find a way to let___ you know___ that

That Thing You Do! - 4 - 1

That Thing You Do! - 4 - 3

From the Motion Picture DOGMA

STILL

Words and Music by
ALANIS MORISSETTE

Tune Guitar:
⑥ = D   ③ = G
⑤ = A   ② = B
④ = D   ① = D

Slowly ♩ = 74

𝄉 *Verses 1 & 4:*

1. I am the harm that you in - flict.
4. I am your trag - e - dy and your for - tune.

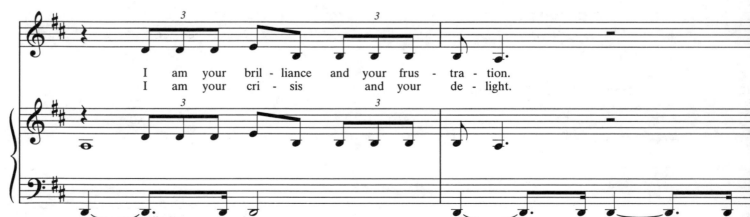

I am your bril - liance and your frus - tra - tion.
I am your cri - sis and your de - light.

*Original recording in D♭.

Still - 7 - 1

I'm the nu - cle - ar bombs if they're to hit.
I am your proph - ets and your prof - its.

I am your im - ma - tur - i - ty and your in - di - gence.
I am your art, I am your bytes.

Verses 2, 3, & 5:

D5

2. I am your mis - fits and your prais - ed.
3. I am your joy and your re - gret.
5. I am your death and your de - ci - sions.

I am your doubt and your con - vic - tion.
I am your fu - ry and your e - la - tion.
I am your pas - sion and your plights.

D.S. ℅ al Coda

⊕ *Coda*

B♭maj7   C   D   Em7

And I love you   still._____
I   see you_____
lie to your coun-

Repeat ad lib. and fade

*First time only.

THAT'S WHAT FRIENDS ARE FOR

Words and Music by
CAROLE BAYER SAGER and BURT BACHARACH

That's What Friends Are For - 3 - 1

THE ENTERTAINER

By SCOTT JOPLIN

Intro:

Not fast

The Entertainer - 4 - 1

Repeat 8va.

The Entertainer - 4 - 2

From the Columbia Motion Picture "ICE CASTLES"

THEME FROM ICE CASTLES

(Through the Eyes of Love)

Lyrics by CAROLE BAYER SAGER

Music by MARVIN HAMLISCH

Theme From Ice Castles - 3 - 1

Theme From Ice Castles - 3 - 2

294

TOMORROW

Lyric by
MARTIN CHARNIN

Music by
CHARLES STROUSE

Tomorrow - 3 - 1

296

(small notes are optional harmony)

Tomorrow - 3 - 2

From the Universal Motion Picture "SCHINDLER'S LIST"

THEME FROM "SCHINDLER'S LIST"

Composed by JOHN WILLIA[M]

Theme From "Schindler's List" - 2 - 1

THEMES FROM "BATMAN FOREVER"

(Main Title/Rooftop Seduction Theme)

Composed by ELLIOT GOLDENTHAL

Themes From "Batman Forever" - 4 - 1

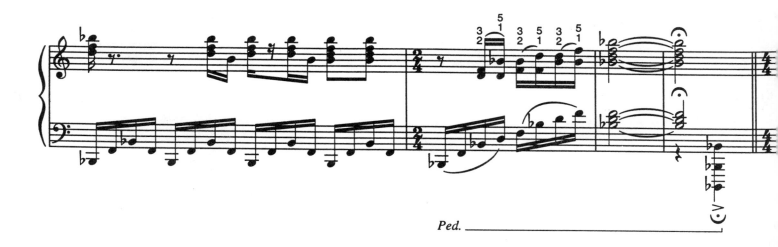

Rooftop Seduction Theme

Sultry & sensuous ♩ = 78

A tempo

THEME FROM INSPECTOR GADGET

Words and Music by
HAIM SABAN and SHUKI LEVY

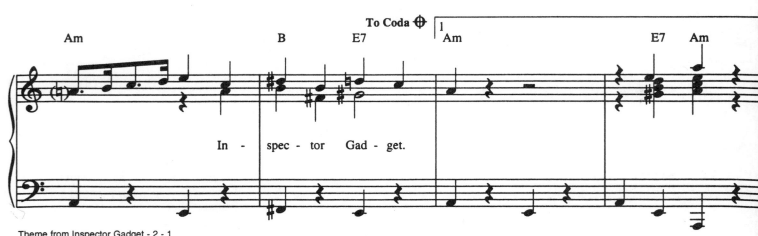

Theme from Inspector Gadget - 2 - 1

Theme From Inspector Gadget - 2 - 2

THEME FROM "JURASSIC PARK"

Composed by
JOHN WILLIAM[S]

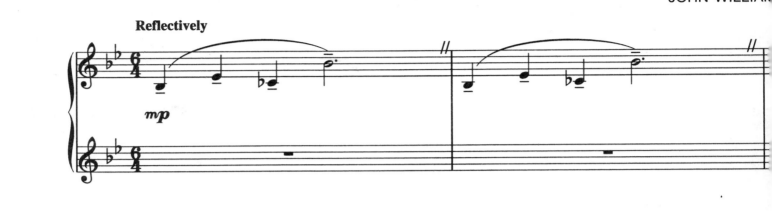

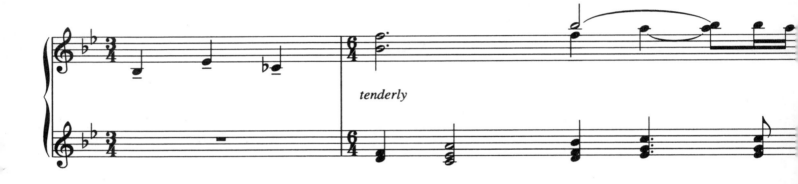

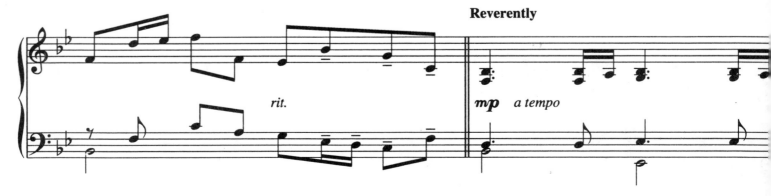

Theme From "Jurassic Park" - 4 - 1

308

From Touchstone Pictures' PEARL HARBOR

THERE YOU'LL BE

Words and Music by
DIANE WARREN

There You'll Be - 5 - 1

TOMORROW NEVER DIES

Words and Music by
SHERYL CROW and MITCHELL FROOM

Tomorrow Never Dies - 7 - 1

Un - til___ that

Coda

eyes._____

Verse 2:
Darling, you've won; it's no fun,
Martinis, girls and guns.
It's murder on our love affair,
But you bet your life, every night
While you're chasing the morning light,
You're not the only spy out there.
It's so deadly, my dear,
The power of wanting you near.
(To Chorus:)

From the Motion Picture "CITY OF ANGELS"

UNINVITED

Words and Music by
ALANIS MORISSETTE

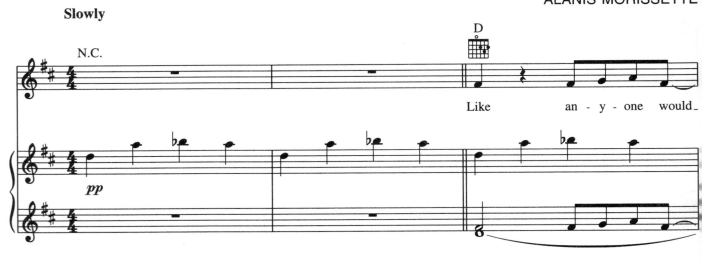

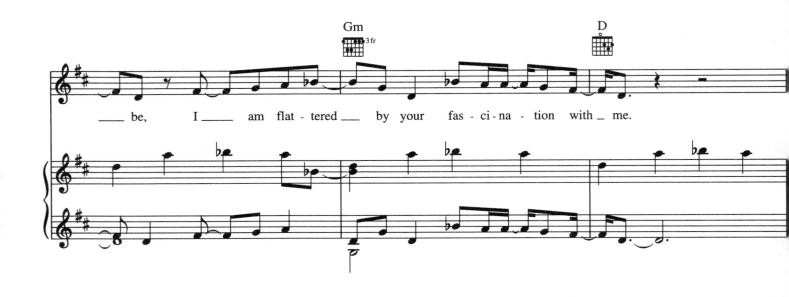

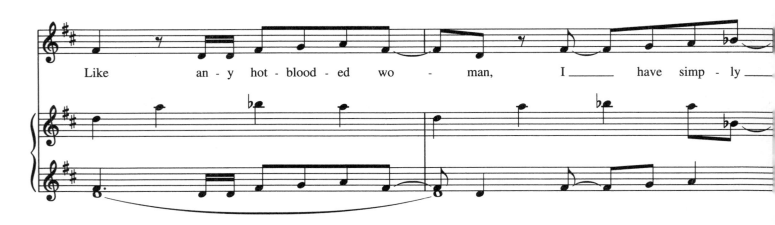

Uninvited - 5 - 1

Gm   D   D7

___ want-ed an ob - ject to crave. ___ But you, you're not al - lowed; ___

G   D

___ you're un - in - vit - ed: an un - for - tu - nate slight.

D

Must be strange-ly ex - cit -
Like an - y un - chart - ed ter -

Gm   D

- ing to ___ watch the sto - ic squirm. ___
- ri - to - ry, I must ___ seem great - ly in - trigu - ing.

From the United Artists Motion Picture "A VIEW TO A KILL"

A VIEW TO A KILL

Words and Music by
DURAN DURAN and JOHN BARRY

Moderately fast (♩ = 132)

1. Meet-ing you___ with a view___ to a kill,___
2. *See additional lyrics*

face to face,___ in se-cret plac - es,___ feel the chill.

A View to a Kill - 5 - 1

kill.

Verse 2:
Choice for you is the view to a kill.
Between the shades, assassination standing still.
The first crystal tears
Fall as snowflakes on your body.
First time in years,
To drench your skin with lovers' rosy stain.
A chance to find a phoenix for the flame,
A chance to die, but can we...
(To Chorus:)

WILD WILD WEST
(Main Theme)

Composed by
ELMER BERNSTEIN

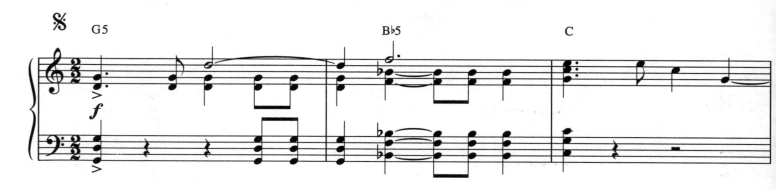

Wild Wild West - 5 - 1

WIN

Words and Music by
BRIAN McNIGHT
and BRANDON BARNES

Win - 5 - 1

THE WIND BENEATH MY WINGS

Words and Music by
LARRY HENLEY and JEFF SILBAR

The Wind Beneath My Wings - 7 - 1

The Wind Beneath My Wings - 7 - 4

You Must Love Me

Lyric by
TIM RICE

Music by
ANDREW LLOYD WEBBER

You Must Love Me - 3 - 1

feel - ing   fright - ened you'll slip   a - way,   you must   love   me,   you must   love   me.

You must   love   me.

Additional Lyrics

Verse 2: *(Instrumental 8 bars)*
Why are you at my side?
How can I be any use to you now?
Give me a chance and I'll let you see how
Nothing has changed.
Deep in my heart I'm concealing
Things that I'm longing to say,
Scared to confess what I'm feeling
Frightened you'll slip away,
You must love me.

From the Warner Bros. Motion Picture THE PERFECT STORM

YOURS FOREVER
(Theme From THE PERFECT STORM)

Music by JAMES HORNER
Lyrics by JOHN MELLENCAMP
and GEORGE GREEN

Yours Forever - 5 - 1

Verse 3:

356